C000059031

AN ARTIST'S LEGACY

There is Hope

AN ARTIST'S LEGACY

There is Hope

A MEMORIAL TO BRENDA JEAN HEFTY

SELECTED POEMS BY BRENDA JEAN HEFTY
PRODUCED BY ERIC MAGELSSEN

PALMETTO
PUBLISHING
Charleston, SC
www.PalmettoPublishing.com

© 2024 by Brenda Jean Hefty

Hardcover ISBN: 979-8-8229-4385-8
Paperback ISBN: 979-8-8229-4386-5

Dedication

This book is dedicated to my departed wife who was a caring and kind individual. Brenda gave hope to many and along with her consummate writing skills, we can now share her artistic abilities with many more.

Acknowledgements

Richard Kehl professor emeritus; University of Washington for his friendship and incredible artistry and poetry and especially for the inspiration to write and create.

The Jensen Beach Flower Club for their love and belief in Brenda along with their good work in helping children and others.

Lilly Hendershot, owner of The Branding Iron, for her creative efforts in the cover design.

Contents

Introduction

Brenda Jean Mayhew was born on December 21,1944 in Brownsville Kentucky in Her grandmother's bed and with the help of a local doctor and her grandmothers Spirited persistence.

They lived in an uninsulated cottage with only a small wood stove for heat on this cold and windy winter night. Her grandfather tended the wood stove for the needed warmth while the doctor and Tinsy worked to entice the large baby out of her mother who was anguished in ever increasing pain due to this large baby girl and once Brenda was born her mother carried this pain with her for every birthday Brenda had, where her mother was present.

Meanwhile her father was at the battlefields of the Second world War in Europe and would not be any part of this until after the war was over and he was back home again.

I came to know and realize Brenda's talents many years ago, when she began to give me a poem she had written for some special occasion, such as valentines day or a birthday. I didn't give more thought beyond my thanking her for such a lovely gift. Over time, and the loss of Brenda's memory from dementia those special gifts ceased to be and yet I kept all of them folded in the jacket of my daily writing journal, so when the thought arrived, I could pull one of them out during my morning ritual of journaling and re-read one and often more of them.

I was in the process of clearing out our home in Florida, since I made the decision to sell it once Brenda had passed.

I came across a stash of twenty poems, most I had not seen, so I immediately sat down and began reading them; this kind of treasure was repeated a number of times, while in the process of preparing the home for sale and since I knew I would be moving back to the Pacific Northwest, I my decided to put all of these found poems along with Brendas few journals and notebooks into their own box for me to revisit once I was living in my new home. When I finally did begin to go through the boxes, I realized Brenda had been writing poetry for many years, having had many varied experiences through travel and family adventures. After so many wonderful finds I came upon the idea to publish her poetry as a memorial.

Brenda was the oldest child of three, born near the end of the Second World War, while her father was still engaged in fighting in Europe. Even though her dad was an officer, he was on the front lines experiencing the horrors of war as all of those there did then. Our society had no understanding of what being involved in such horrific events did to the front-line soldiers then, so they when returned back home it was assumed those experiences would go away.

Now couple this with coming home to a family and new responsibilities, there and in her fathers case having grown up in a family with a physically abusive father, which brought about some deep seeded psycological trouble that would haunt her father for most of his life, along with having re-percussions on this new young family. Brendas father may have tried to manage his anger yet could not hold back the pangs from his experiences both growing up and then in a war no one wanted, but had to fight. As a result the oldest child became the recipient of his outbursts and his anger.

Brenda's grandmother and her mothers genetic gifts were well entrenched within this sweet child and with high intelligence along with a very strong spirit, she weathered these storms. Brenda was an A student and a sweet and kind individual, always striving for excellence in whatever she did at home or school. This was not without losing the ability to find her passions and to see them through, since her father's chastising her for being proud of some accomplishment she had done, was aways a part of his way rearing her. Brenda never gave up on her passion for the arts, yet she stopped showing any outward emotion, no matter how well something she accomplished was received by others. Years later Brenda sat down, compiled a list of her fathers transgressions, put them in a letter and presented this to her now very senior father. Her letter was a letter of forgiveness.

Now, in his late eighties he received the letter with gentle tears flowing and they made their peace finally and for good.

Before Brenda and I were married she said to me there was only one stipulation that she had for marrying, which was to move from the northwest to Florida to be near her mother and father during their final years, so that we could help them.

Brenda had already shared many of her experiences growing up ,and wanting to be a singer, a musician or an artist of some kind, although none ever materialized,so we agreed to settle near her mom and dad as well as her brother and his wife where we spent most of the next twenty years living in Jensen Beach Florida.

This book is a memorial to Brenda Jean Hefty an in the last ten years of her life she fought and struggled with dementia, that was eventually determined to be Lewybody dementia.

A Childs Gift
In the Words of Her Mother...

Drifting in a warm current,
waking as your blondness lights
the morning clouds,

We move through the simple moments
like dolphins playing in slow motion.

Space and time are the ocean
we float on as we'd raise a sail
to reflect the glow of our contentment.

Roaming beaches of the past,
I will return with shells
of our sea dreams,

And place them along a path
leading to the lighthouse I have built
to show you the way home.

Accidental Beauty

Twelve small hairs spread in a perfectly spaced pattern
Across the temple of a young man playing his guitar
And singing his heart out in front of 30,000 people
Surely, must be recognized as beauty.

Those twelve hairs were curved uniformly in a design
That would have been the envy of envy of an ancient Greek
Sitting in the shade of a fig tree
While he carved a stone lintel

The small miracle of happenstance
transmitted by modern technology
Makes us wonder what it takes to mystify the mind.
For the observer who is stimulated by a
reverie of cause and effect
At work in human evolution. is it the question...
What is the ultimate power of human consciousness?

Is it the ability to create the grandiose inventions that
Literally change our world?

Or the ability to recognize the presence of
accidental beauty?

A Conversation with Your Self

As a child you grew
and didn't know the growing.
You made choices
and didn't choose the knowing.
You gave little thought
to the gift you were giving.
Were you less aware
of the life you were living?

You were taught that pleasing
others was absolutely the best.
It was so uncouth to disappear
and not think of the rest.
Remember? - always feeling
you were being put to a test?

Where is the balance?
How do you trust
what you are doing
to be simply a must?

Fill your life with alternatives?
Receive the gift commitment gives?
Prolong the search for what so deeply lives?
It's time to float out of the mental maze
and into the weightless is.

A Day to Live Over

A picture-window sunrise was seen but not felt.
Words were chosen over action.
Unneeded sleep abused inner harmony.
Criticism became a shortcut to failure.
A good heart played hide and seek.
Robbery was committed by a reasonable choice.
Rightness drove away from beauty and freedom.

The loss of that day is mourned
like the loss of a lover.

A Familiar Hand

Don't go.
Listen to the pulse
we have in common.
Let us share the alchemy
of the present, and believe
that thought is not measured by time.

I want to stay.
Feeling snowed in by flakes
that melt as they fall,
hear me as I call.

If life has its moments,
then let this be ours,
to share the closeness of separation.

A Fond Memory

Snow melting underfoot
to reveal sand beneath the pines
at a mountain lake.

Brenda Jean Hefty

A Love Letter

Wood hitting metal, no human cry,
just wood hitting metal in damp darkness.
We don't talk enough to suit me.
Our dogs know each other better.

Yet somehow those sticks I found
on the sidewalk in the morning
bore your intensity of only hours before.
My scream became your echo.

You use edges to define yourself,
and that moment of being on edge
brought us to toe on the same note,
just like two ballerinas.

Want to arm wrestle?
Want to spit in my face?
Want to delight in our abundance
Together?

A Loving Business

It's true she has another mental hobby,
but this time she knows it.
She is planning to open a gallery for
the martial arts.

She envisions an ambience not unlike
the best of evenings you have spent with her.

Silken robes take their places in an.
antique armoire while the fragrance
of flowers or tea brewing fills the air.

She hunts for treasures to fill the
awaiting shelves, but sadly wonders
where she can find a supply of those
simple attentions you give when least
expected but truly needed.

Will her customers detect that subtle
tone of desire in your voice should she
record you reading to her from a favorite story?

How will she convey the communion she has felt in a
massage that began as a shoving match.

And does she dare to frame and display
such a personal collection of pictures?

Of course, she's relieved when reminded
the gallery is an exercise in fantasy.
But she still believes it would be worth
exposing herself and you this way if she
Could learn something from the curious
who would enter such a domain - something
that would deepen her understanding of those arts.

It's true, she's looking for a fair exchange
Again.

A Precious Realization

She wanted to awaken at 6:00 this morning
Using that internal mechanism that works without
The need of an electric hum or pretimed music.
But when she opened her eyes,
Her ears said she was still dreaming.
It sounded like a mountain speaking with violent
Eloquence, then a flash revealed the reality.
It was an event which happens seldom in her area -
Only twice before in the past SO years during
the Month of July.
She listened for the drops to hit the porch,
Still disbelieving there was any need to gather in
The chairs, cushions and towels she had left.
Later when each person she met described his own version
Of waking at 6:00 a.m. she was reminded of how little
Attention she had given to such a rare occurrence,
And now she wants it replayed tomorrow complete with
Birdsong in anticipation and pitted dust as aftermath.
Letting go of this fantasy, she feels the warmth of
Gratitude ascend within.
She had spent an entire day in the absence of her
Mate and child now suddenly realizes in a world of
Many gifts, they are the most precious.

Brenda Jean Hefty

A Small Death

Yesterday I told you I didn't look at you enough.
I thought of making a yellow dress with an outline of your
tiny silhouette repeated across the bodice.

Today I touched your soft, warm body just long enough
to feel the last heartbeat.
I jerked my hand away, stunned.
You had hardly struggled.
I never knew you were so fragile.
The strength of your song was deceiving.

That moment replayed as often as I did my own
ice-bound form of flying.
Then I noticed my hair was drying like two small wings
behind my ears.
Flap your wings you say. Okay.

Your empty cage will hang outside my window.
As it spins slowly in the breeze, I will tell myself,
"I'm on my own now. It's time to sing my own songs."

A Social Disease

The numbness starts in the bones.
In her case, the lower jaw.
Yet, she leads with her chin.

It is a chin that shows the result
of a disease that lies dormant
beneath the skin, awaiting the
perfect conditions.

When she has gone too long,
inviting the ecstasy of human contact,
forgetting the necessary precautions,
the growth emerges.

Still perplexed by the teachings
contrasting selfish with selfless,
she cautions those closest to her
about the contagion.

"You can catch it from me.
And it has several forms -
One affects the genitals."

For her it is part of the price
she is willing to pay.
The lesions are a nuisance,
but it is the numbness she fears.
Keeping it localized and brief
is her desire.

It is a small bribe,
holding off the threatened
loss of life.

She is not about to change.
The look in her eyes is the wisdom
of one who holds an infirmity dear.

Brenda Jean Hefty

A Tale of Redemption and Trancendance

The female heart pumps to fill the womb,
but even so we don't understand the flow.
Feeling cursed as well as blessed,
we can't hear the plaintive echo
whispering the pride and beauty of venus.

Where is the tide that has to decide
to be released against the shore?
How many fishes do we know
who close their mouths so as to slow
the mingling of the blood and the water?

Does it take a tempest to rise,
Bringing fierce winds to blow
a sea-change into our lives?
When will we find a welcome within
that simply allows all to begin?

Whether or not magic is the key
is a difference of feeling for you and me.
We must start back at the heart
on our life's most ardent journey
to reach the center of this world's body.

The next step relates to the mind
and how it leads us from behind.
We must make of it a gate,
open to our path and all we may find.

Should we go further a fiery test is next,
for in that wondrous center also burns a fear of sex,
inhabited by serpent demons of every size.
The letting go of muscles that hold tight the thighs
brings an upward rush of feeling for the heart to realise.

A Winter Swim

Jake the snake has staked his claim
upon a November beach.
A thin line draws us to his heart
lying before a blood red sunset
dying over a becalmed sea.

Brenda Jean Hefty

A Writer's Plea

Learn by teaching
Listen to your own advice
Don't stand idly by while someone is sinking
The life on the line maybe your own

It seems to me the trees living in the cities
all grow to be the same height,
as if the air is too heavy to allow
them to attain their differences

An Evening Out

There is something immense about the
loneliness that exists in the crowded
space arranged for a party of strangers
who live side by side.

If they were there to be absorbed by each other,
air would not be the main element.
The way it holds a charge and conducts
vibration always interferes,

Such effort calls for a magician from the sea
to reveal the passage that water makes
through a gill, and that trust doesn't suspend
a whale hundreds of feet above the ocean floor.

Does the pain of resistance that enters
the soul via the lung hearken back to
that first amphibian's breath?
Are we so far from a liquid language?

By the By

Have you noticed there are words, phrases,
that follow you through your whole life,
popping up every now and then?
They are like toddlers at your heels mumbling
in their effort to form a new language.
Most of the time you pay little attention
to their presence because you are preoccupied.

Then one day you stop in your tracks;
turn to look down and ask, "What was that you said?"
Suddenly you want to know the relevance of
these little expressions because you recognize
they are part of the puzzle of your being.

At four in the morning you are wide awake,
searching for the avenue (the Oxford Dictionary?)
that will provide the meaning, a definition,
so you can go back to sleep, or get on with
your treadmill of activity.

Perhaps we are each a receiver for whispers
from the Universe, sent to remind us
we are not just toiling individuals,
but also integral parts of a magnificent, enormous
whole that, by the by, cannot operate without us.

P.S The Universe is using me to whisper this.

Captain oh Captain

You resisted the invitation of a
soothing bath to the accompaniment of the waves.
You laughed when I said you were a mighty man.
And all the while we were under
the shelter of Neptune.

No singing springs offered the water I poured
over your head, yet as you raised and looked
at me, the droplets in your hair and beard
caused tears to flow in my eyes.

I saw the god in you, and felt the weight of
your footsteps in the sand.
The boat we watched at dawn leaving the harbour
took your heart out to sea and your memory back
more than a decade.

If I could summon the power of Poseidon
I would have him arrange a life for you
aboard a dawn treader (uninhabited by the ghost
Of your father) that would carry you into the
light of each new day, as a captain finally
aware of his own command

Coming Home

Can it be the mind feels the gravity
of a drop of rain that falls from the
top of an ancient tall tree far more
than a drop from the sky?

Can it slow the being to a point of
awareness to imagine such an arboreal
descent whispering, "there is no time
like the present"?

And while answering yes, has the cage
been erected to house the wild animal
of experience?

The trainer who has done so is sure
to have her life spark dampened as
the lion changes into an overgrown
house cat.

Dilemma

Standing at the kitchen window right before sunset,
Watching the trunks of madronas and cedars
Shimmer with iridescent light,
The same old pressure occurs - do something!
The magic will end momentarily.

Such torture to have free time to watch the light go.
Turning now to face the sun as it hangs
Just above the hills, I am challenged.
Do I walk away before the sun sets?
The thought brings on feelings of disrespect.

But the longer I watch the sun flickering
Through the trees, gleaming off the water,
The more embarrassed and humble I feel.

What creation do I have to offer
That justifies my being to even a minute
Fraction of the power and majesty
I am watching?

No wonder priests have been raising infants
Up to the sky since ancient times
As if to proclaim "This is our Shining Light!"

Down Home

They always washed their feet
and sprinkled talc in their sandals
before they went to town.
For me it was a time to sit
and watch and ask childish questions.

What a sorority they had -
My two aunts, my grandmother
And Mary, my mom.
Each summer was another pledging
to keep the distances in tact.

I didn't see that then.
So many of us sleeping so close -
breathing in each other's sighs,
snapping beans on the back porch,
I didn't recognize the lies-.

I only wanted watermelon on
the 4th of July and thunderstorms
that kept us suspended
until the sun came out;
and boy cousins with baseball muscles
who would play hide and seek
in the courthouse yard at night.

I still love saying I was born
in Kentucky near the Cave
where the Green River is brown
and women wash their feet
before they go to town.

Dreaming Magically

There once was a woman
with a floral tattoo on her right breast.
She used to swim nude in the backwaters,
exposing herself like a dolphin
surfacing backward.

Men who couldn't resist her
would jump into the water to touch her.
As each one came close to her,
she would turn him around,
and taste his hair.

If the hair passed her test,
she would cut some off,
and later sell it to people who believed
it helped them make magic.

This beautiful woman supported herself
With the hair men surrendered.

Perhaps this is what wise women
have always done...
.. .appear vulnerable, act quickly to disarm men,
And help create magic in the world.

Brenda Jean Hefty

Fathering

When did you choose to be a father?
Think of that moment, that flicker.
And hold your breath.
It's no distance at all.
You needn't keep the thrill a secret,
Like a mustard seed in a glass bubble.
Now is the time for a cartwheel or somersault.
Spin around and feel the shimmer of the
King's jewels sewn into your clothing.
Thrust that inner wind over your vocal chords
And vibrate to the song of self.

Your love is like the water of a spring.
See yourself floating on this water.
Choose a boat to carry your gifts.
Teach your child to navigate the boat.
Let him show you the spot on the map.
Tell him it is only a heartbeat away.
And feel your heart beat.

Flowers Grow in the Dirt

You resisted the invitation of a
Soothing bath to the accompaniment of the waves.
You laughed when I said you are a mighty man.
And all the while we had surrendered ourselves
to the shelter of Neptune.

No singing springs offered the water I poured
over your head, yet as you raised and looked
at me, the droplets in your hair and beard
caused tears to flow in my eyes.

I see the god in you, and whether you ask
for them or not, I will continue to bring
those flowers that I find growing everywhere
in the dirt.

For David

We're still on that beach
where the tideline is masked
by millions of tiny deaths,
and a black dog barks at the daredevil
taking his biplane into loops overhead.

You want to see the light
through the wave crests,
and I can't see beyond
the wasted life at my feet.

Energy greets you there.
A sealion surfaces to get his bearing
and becomes your discovery.
You run with a cadence set by the surf.

In me, you have chosen your opposite.
My vision of subtraction can be an ebb
for your positive flow,
and my burning doesn't have to unsettle
your quiet depths.

Why do you think there have always
been bonfires on the beach at night?
Where water lies cold under the dark,
flame cajoles a place of warmth
within it.

I as the Dividing Line

This language finds me in between,
standing on the single letter that
forms the single word that aligns
itself with the poles.

I can form a dam in the middle of
a positive flow.
I can be convinced that only the
negative is at work.
And only I can turn sideways to act
as a valve for this rush of feeling
that keeps me alive.

Imaginary Shore leave

You resisted the invitation of a
soothing bath to the accompaniment of the waves.
You laughed when I said you were a mighty man.
And all the while we were under the shelter of
Neptune.

No singing springs offered the water I poured
over your head, yet as you raised and looked
at me, the droplets in your hair and beard
caused tears to flow in my eyes.

I saw the god in you, and felt the weight of
his footsteps in the sand.
The boat we watched at dawn leaving the harbour
took your heart out to sea and your memory back
more than a decade.

If I could summon the power of Poseidon
I would have him arrange a life for you
Aboard a dawn treader (uninhabited by the spirit
of your father) that would carry you into the
light of each new day, as a captain
aware of his own command.

I'M ONLY HUMAN

Says, don't expect too much of me,
I'm not God, yet it belittles.
What ancient someone was relieved
to see himself as inferior?

The Greeks at least were clever in fashioning
Their gods and goddesses complete with imperfections.
Those deities proved to be vain, jealous,
greedy, lustful, and manipulative.

They were accorded the flaws of humans
who have everything but aren't satisfied.
Greek wisdom and need combined to project
a magnificent mirror of awareness.

How strange, the Jews produced
a perfect god in human form.
No wonder they didn't accept their own creation.
We've all been on edge ever since.

If we have come to an age of accepting
our own internal higher self,
then perhaps we can change the phrase to
"I'm wondrously human."

Is Gravity Truly Perpendicular to the Horizon?

What you say goes - but only for you and those
who agree with you.
So, is gravity truly perpendicular to the horizon?

If she wasn't Joan of Arc,
then she was the Old Woman in the Shoe,
and if she wasn't the old woman,
then she was Gwenivere dancing
with the virgins in May.

Fire was her element
and she had always been a crusader.
In fact, the campaigns were too few.
It was difficult for her to remain patient,
and that was when she became the old woman.

Complaints about her confinement
and her ragtag children were pointless.
So, off she would go to her closet
and pull out the silkiest thing she had,
then whistle her way down to frolic in the meadow.

As Gwenivere she was superb, the king agreed,
barring the facination with Lancelot, of course.
Arthur so wanted order and his offspring
so wanted the throne, the poor gal was doomed.
Once again she donned the shining armour.

Surely, she could create the ideal
if she wanted to, you say.
Possibly she was perfect at any given moment,
intensely pursuing the illusive, magical sound
that would elicit an echo from life's mountain.

Isn't it Enough...

To watch the sun make its slow plunge
Creating color and softness in the Western Clouds
While we enjoy the cardinals visiting the feeder
And finish a carefully crafted meal.

Do we have to press ourselves to find proof
That our ideas and dreams are superior
To what has been or is being accepted?
Is the competitive edge where our worth exists?

Is personal contentment completely passe'?
Where are the awards for keeping to oneself.
Being introspective finding peace of my mind?

Brenda Jean Hefty

KING COBRA

King Cobra does not bite,
He seduces his chosen one.
With his hood spread and his eyes diamond bright,
He calls her from the harem -
Come be my slave, share my den and keep me company.

He moves to her rhythm, making it his own.
Slowly hypnotizing his captive until
She steadily bends backward,
lifting her perfect wound
for him to see and approve.

King Cobra says come, ride my soft tail.
Let me hold you, sweet asp, in my teeth.
Don't pull away until we see the sun transcend the horizon.
Let me paralyze you with ecstasy.

Join me on the open road,
with nothing but the future ahead.
I'll be your lover, you be my queen.
Find your destiny in my sting.

Leap Year Transition

Appreciation for the Cat's moon shadow
Jupiter, Venus and Mars rendezvous again in 150 years
Heartbreak sung and danced to, but unfelt
green eyes of a sister's love
asexual fingers stretch to make friends with the guitar
Hugs and Kisses -what do you know, our needs agree
You go your way, I'll go mine
Fates, Furies, not we three, just birds of a feather are we
Daddy dear, they operated on your heart, yet I am healing

Lunch with an expectant father whose unconscious reveals
The tight collar he wears. He eats and says yes a lot -
What an agreeable fellow.
Six minute tunnel to the continent's edge where the warnings
beckon and a rock rhinocerous that I'll see in
my dreams, watches as my back to the cliff stiffens slightly
in a lovers embrace.
Show me your disappointment, it may change my mind.
In the realm of the senses, a gift of time. Such a special place
in which to admit you are Yin, I am Yang.

Traveling home with a moon rainbow over my right shoulder.
Read me a story about a snake. Yes, the one that starts
with Pierre making love to a dead naiad.
How to describe a love that combines fire and water? Does
it simply work hard, like steam, or is it meant to purify?
I promise not to burn you if you promise not to put me out.

Learning to Relax

Poetry is my way of handling my
Intense sense of involvement and
Responsibility.

The sister inside who seemed for so
Many years to be pointing the critical
Finger, I now realize, has been pointing
To the pen.

Recently each time I have found myself
Uncomfortably alone, I have known it is
Time for a poem. I don't have to make
The choice to write, just be aware of
My own discomfort.

In the past this sent me into a panic,
Fearing I would abuse the gift of time.
I find I am learning to relax into my
Own emptiness and not struggle to fill
It with physical excess.

Living with the Incurable (I)

Haven't they always said,
"There's nothing you can do."

One moment you're drifting in your own dream.
The next, you're pushing a wheelchair
down hospital halls, singing ditties
and smiling at everyone who passes.

(Not a day goes by that your heart
doesn't' fly to distant romantic places.)

The child just IS.
It's you the parent who has the handicap,
who has been trapped by the word "normal",
snared by the term "acceptance"

Now you must learn the language of being -
Together, parent and child,
Tending the garden of no reason.

Brenda Jean Hefty

Living with the Incurable (II)

Bitch, bitch, bitch.
No money again.
Promises, promises, promises.
Be patient and forgiving.

He asks too much of you.
Like the drunk on the street -
'Give me another dime
and a little more time."

You're married, of course,
And that leads to divorce.
After all, he's done it to you,
Now you can say, 'I'm through!"

It's time to turn around,
find a new friend.
Establish the ritual ground,
so you can do it all again.

It's a sickness called "blame" -
A worldwide plague of agonizing pain.
It causes people to die while still walking.
It lives deep in our hearts,
and is heard daily in our talking.

Religious myths like Eve and her apple
allow us to claim,
"Someone else made us do it."

What we create
needn't come back as hate -
for ourselves or others.
Paying attention without judging
has rewards we've yet to discover.

Margin for Safety

I arrive and you buckle up,
saying, "Experience has taught you
to use these things."

Maybe that experience was the message,
"There will always be rough spots
in the road."

Funny though,
those rough spots appear so close
to the most distracting beauty.

Brenda Jean Hefty

Morning of Gratitude

Five white boats drift with the tide early this
first day of September,
Their owners patiently awaiting the strike of a
Pacific Northwest salmon
While the water they glide upon mirrors the sun reflected off the
houses on shore,
And Mozart's third violin concerto plays on my
small compact disc player,
And I think about the drawing rooms of the aristocracy
where Mozart
First played his notes that connect us to the sublime.

What a wonder the Universe is to have delivered this heavenly
sound Through the centuries to anyone in the world to enjoy -
No longer just for privileged ears.
Dare we take it for granted in the same way we barely notice
The sun reflecting off the houses mirrored in the
calm water of morning?

My Own Connection

No one tells me when I am on.
The stars won't turn another color
for the benefit of my cue to enter.
A white light of benevolence must
generate from my own imagination.
This road was created from the inspiration
of many, but only I must take it.

A man made machine stands illumined
between me and the sea, like a black
and chrome sculpture, save for my
day-long ride on its back.
Vibrations still pulse from the
base of my spine, and my crotch is
newly alive.

This man who asks me for the time of day,
has just given me the time of my life.
And now I know that my reality will
allow me to create a dream, but to
whom do I say thank you?

Nature Talking

A sore neck can bring the sudden
realization that it takes an act of God
to hold one's head up.

Natures Mystery

There is something immense about the
loneliness that exists In the crowded
space arranged for a party of strangers
who live side by side.

If they were there to be absorbed by each other,
air would not be the main element.
The way it holds a charge and conducts
vibration always interferes.

Such effort calls for a magician from the sea
To reveal the passage that water makes
Through a gill, and that trust doesn't suspend
A whale hundreds of feet above the ocean floor.

Does the pain of resistance that enters
the soul via the lung hearken back to
that first amphibian's breath?
Are we so far from a liquid language?

Brenda Jean Hefty

Observations of a Wedding

My son stands with his back to me
At the altar with his bride.
He is turning toward a new life
And must keep his eyes aside.

Something from the Bible comes back
To me about a man...
He must leave his mother
And cleave unto his wife.

When he told me he wanted to marry
I said, "Of course, it seems right."
He smiled at those words -
Longed for approval, a light.

Now I want to take them back,
Gather them into the pit of my selfishness
As something to quiet the cry in the night
From the dream that confuses.

One Moment Please

You wanted to awaken at 6:00 this morning,
using that internal mechanism that works without
the need of an electric hum or pretimed music.
But, when you opened your eyes,
your ears said you were still dreaming.

It sounded like a mountain speaking with violent eloquence
then a flash revealed the reality.
It was an event which happens seldom in your area -
only twice before in the last 50 years during
the month of July.

You listened for the drops to hit the porch,
still disbelieving there was any need to gather in
the chairs, cushions and towels you left there so brazenly.

Later, when each person you met described his own version
of waking at 6:00 a.m. you were reminded of how little
attention you gave to such a rare occurrence,
and now you want it replayed tomorrow, complete with
birdsong in anticipation and pitted dust as aftermath.

Letting go of this fantasy, you feel the warmth
of gratitude ascend within.
You have spent an entire day in the absence of your
mate and child realizing in a world of many gifts,
they are the most precious.

ONE NIGHT ON THE COAST

There were foghorns that night,
but they collided anyway.
Two different personalities
performing very different rites of passage
at the western edge of the continent.

The fog was unpredictable
they were stereotypical.
Trapped by their human legacy -
Male vs. Female, Youth vs. Age,
Energy vs. Wisdom, Love vs. Friendship.

Creating a new dimension
and the measure for it
is their task post collision.
No manner of truth will be used
to alienate a perfect decision.

Will they appear in the headlines?
Probably not, but in their place,
a story of coastal residents
awakened in their beds,
relieved to find only fog horns
disturbing the midnight air.

One Day a Year?

When did you choose to be a father?
Think of that moment, that flicker,
and hold your breath.
It's no distance at all.
You needn't keep the thrill a secret,
like a mustard seed in a glass bubble.
Now is the time for a cartwheel or somersault.
Spin around and feel the shimmer of the
King's jewels sewn into your clothing.
Thrust that inner wind over your vocal chords
And vibrate to the song of Self.

Your love is like the water of a spring.
See yourself floating on this water.
Choose a boat to carry your gifts.
Teach your child to navigate the boat.
Let him show you the spot on the map.
Tell him it is only a heartbeat away,
And feel your heart beat.

Peace Performance

The man stood in front of a cheering crowd
of perhaps a thousand fans.
He had an acoustical guitar hanging
from a strap over his shoulder.

The crowd quieted as he began to strum
a familiar tune.
He sang about a black bird singing
in the dead of night

It was a simple song coming from
an aging voice, played without flourish.
The audience cheered with an enthusiasm
that brought tears to the eyes.

This was praise for the human spirit,
the perseverance of creativity,
and the ability to love oneself.

Is it possible that music is the single
most powerful medium supporting
world peace?

Realization

She wanted to awaken at 6:00 this morning,
using that internal mechanism that works without
the need of an electric hum or pretimed music.
But when she opened her eyes,
her ears said she was still dreaming.
It sounded like a mountain speaking with violent
eloquence, then a flash revealed the reality.
It was an event which happens seldom in her area -
only twice before in the last 50 years during the
month of July.

She listened for the drops to hit the porch,
still disbelieving there was any need to gather in
the chairs, cushions and towels she had left.

Later when each person she met described his own
version of waking at 6:00 a.m. she was reminded of how
little attention she had given to such a rare occurrence,
and now she wants it replayed tomorrow complete with
birdsong in anticipation and pitted dust as aftermath.

Letting go of this fantasy, she feels the warmth of
gratitude ascend within.
She had spent an entire day in the absence of her
mate and child now suddenly realizes in a world of
many gifts, they are the most precious.

She Doesn't Call Her Stella Anymore

She's on her way to heaven,
But won't open the door.
She's fought ecstasy for ninety years,
And won't give in for many more.

Letting go will be the last thing
My grandma Tincy does.
Perhaps she doesn't know
That's all there ever was.

Born in her bed,
My cheek against muslin she had sown,
Bonded to her shelf-like bosom,
I inherited iron, feathers and stone.

I'm not ungrateful for the inheritance,
Just expectant for the day I let that be.
And find a silk dress to wear when I go dancing
With the smell of jasmine on me.

She said, "Just Be Yourself"

She couldn't have known how hard that is for me.
Now if she had said, "Pretend you are a stone",
I would be there still sitting on the beach,
smooth, relaxed, not needing or caring.

Or, if she had suggested I see the world from
a bird's eye in flight over the estuary,
I would feel a sudden rush of air through
my armpit hairs and my head would tilt to one side
as the reeds parted for a flash of silver.

From satyrs and centaurs to Caliban and Dracula,
an array of half human, half animal beings
who were and still are - with us.
Shakespeare must have been.
He wrote so eloquently of the struggle.

Unwinding my past, dreaming my future,
what a daily ritual, but to let go and just be...
Or, maybe it is to take hold and just be.
This seems to be life's greatest dare.

Oh, to be a daredevil!

Brenda Jean Hefty

SANS SOUCI of the Montana Wilderness

Where are your secrets?
Built by firemen with town wives,
you were sold to a Swedish man and woman
who brought the finest from their homeland
to create themselves in you.
And when they left, they left everything.
You became their monument.

To stay within your log walls
and listen to the antique clock
compete with the stream outside for the time's measure
is to place oneself gracefully in the moment
of life's passage.

My mind wants to make of you a bridge
holding past and future
as the secure walls for this chasm
called the present.

And all the while the antlers
hanging from the garden gate,
the birch rocker before the hearth,
and oil chandelier suspended in your parlor
keep whispering without breath,
"acceptance is your only choice."

Siamese Twins

They were joined at the heart, and to make matters
Worse, they weren't of the same sex.
It had seemed normal enough when they were younger.
They had grown up with the same fascinations.
For some time now they knew they looked at life
Differently, and were able to laugh when each
moved in the opposite direction at the at the same time.

It was she who noticed the loneliness first.
He was content and continued to praise her beauty
and strength. But when she mentioned the word "Mother"
the heat of his anger gave her a fever.
He said her warnings sounded like threats, but
swallowing her fear only led to her vomiting.
He began to wonder when the dogs had abandoned Pompeii,
and became uneasy about what he knew best- patience.

Secretly neither wanted to give up the warmth.
Slowly guilt joined their company to form a menage a trois.

Couldn't a choice made prior to birth be altered?
Cellular structure suspended in simultaneous time
must be vulnerable to belief?

What more natural place for them to reside now than
where the earth was gradually opening each day,
spreading and dividing.
Their neighbors were metaphsycians, astrologers, healers,
alchemists, yet no prism hung in their window, and
crystal was something they drank from.

It began with an invitation from a woman with a child
at her breast who had chosen to mute her vision.
Would they join an experiment in power on the night
of the full moon? It was obvious she was making a
break with the slavetrader.
Tempted but skeptical, the change was delayed.

Though her head buzzed from the pull
of the power she was not fully in touch with, her fear was
assuaged by touching the smooth the smooth talisman of her
sexuality.

STOP IN THE NAME OF NATURE!

Last night as the sun was making a fiery plunge into the horizon,
I ran to the garage, took down my bicycle from its hook
And began to ride west.

To my surprise even the eastern sky was hot pink.

I rode toward the highway
Wondering why I could still hear cars and trucks.
The sky was so startling,
Surely traffic would have come to a halt.

Instead it was as if nothing was happening,
Which made me wonder ...
What is happening to us?

Do we really feel nothing unless
directed by a screen projecting
the latest melodramatic "B" movie?

Do we no longer know when to stop,
When to be amazed and exhilarated?
Is the agenda we set on a daily basis
so important we can't pause for five minutes
to observe a momentary miracle of natural beauty?

Is this the indifference that has allowed us
to ignore the well being of our planet?
What remedy can we create that will
bring back the ability to care?

What if the amount of time we spent watching
raindrops on the surface of a lake
were greater than our daily absorption
with the internet or TV?

Do we have to give up technology
to regain our place in Nature?
Sounds far fetched when
We aren't even willing to give up plastic bags!

Struck by You

Pinned to the velvet
with wings still fluttering.
Mind riding a carousel
with machinery stuttering.
Body aglow from heart to skin.
Makes me wonder how to allow
the dream to begin.

Adrift on an ocean
in a boat with one oar.
Called to be rational
from an illogical shore.
Is the magic of this moment
a game we create
to bridge the gap in how to relate?

How many times will we practice?
To the others, what will we say?
Is it pretense or protection we foster?
Either or neither, have we lost our way?

Is this moment important -
Is it a test?
Are we paying attention,
or taking a rest?

I know I am struck by you,
And don't know what to do.
Longing for an answer,
it is the questions I pursue.

Just know this - given the chance,
I will stand up with you.
I am happy to know you
the way that I do.

Brenda Jean Hefty

The Calling

Death was a patient visitor
Sitting at my father's feet,
Reaching out often
For the hand my father offered.

Gently, I would return my father's hand
To rest in his lap.
"Not yet", I would say to him,
As I lifted a strawberry to his lips.

Come back to your senses... stay,
Look to the sky, smell the evergreens,
Feel this lotion that soothes your skin.
Don't leave us while we yearn to restore you.

But, like the tide pulled by the full moon,
He couldn't resist.
In a brief, unprotected moment,
Death moved from his feet to his heart.

I will never again feed him another strawberry,
Or listen to his lectures, or put my head on his chest.
He is with his Lord and with those who
Called to him from the other side, saying,
"Come, we yearn to restore you."

The Delay

The room held the crowd
the way an oven holds a pie
on the verge of being overcooked.

The waiting for someone to come
and whisk open the door,
kept the heat on.

No one cried though,
that is, no one over three feet tall,
and popcorn kept most of them quiet.

We all sort of expected it,
you know, inertia, forgetfulness,
and losing card games made sense.

Loss doesn't have to look like
something burned, and gain
doesn't always feel like speed.

It's very possible we'll never know
just what it is we need.

The Dream

The dream began at the end of a road.
Coming to the top of a hill on smooth pavement,
rounding a curve, preparing to accelerate to
optimum enjoyment and suddenly boulders lay
in the way.
Deja vu had saved them from catastrophe,
but must their life together ever be so?

An alternate route took them to a man
who offered a glass of pleasant liquid.
They chatted sociably, indifferently until
it was time to go, then her desire to be funny,
her need to be recognized, caused her to flounder
on her words, "thank you for the enjoyable 5 ½ inches."

It was at that point she knew she was dreaming.
She tried to retrieve the confusion, but it was too late.
Why was her longing always so evident?
When would she see the day when the emptiness
would seem poignant instead of hellish?

Outside he was calling to her from a car
with their child in the front seat.
(They had arrived on bicycles, traveling in
the open air.)
She felt strange as she considered what appeared
to be a container,
And he continued to call her name even as
he watched her approach.

The End of a Hummingbird Summer

September 29th and the first storm of Fall
brought rain through the day and into the night.
The tidal channel is brimming,
The flowers are sadly drooping,
And the hummingbirds are nowhere in sight.

All summer those miniature flying acrobats
Bombarded our ears with high powered wing vibrations.
Filling the sky before our eyes,
They fought over the flow of sugar water,
With "cheet, cheet" warnings of territorial rights

Our own movements came to mirror theirs -
Darting an island, then off; to the airport, then home;
To the mountains, then to the sea; to the doctor,
To the cemetery, then back to life -
Joyous with friends and family.
The abundance was unsettling.
The frenzy and mix could have curdled cream.

September came glowing golden each day,
With nothing holding back the door from closing.
It was coming to an end.
Yet in the quiet moments there was a whisper ...
"pay attention, memories are the precious afterlife"

The hummingbirds will make their journey south
And we will travel just as far to stay warm,
To rejoin the flock we left behind,
To defy time and space,
To be filled with the nectar of existence,
And to pay attention to each shinning moment

The First Prayer

Let me open a window
for breezes to enter my life
bringing scents of beauty,
and peace and joy
Let the simple sounds arrive
to sooth
longing that isn't understood
and revive my sleepy spirit
Let me bury pain and sorrow
with past memories and learn
to forgive myself as I forgive
others - by opening a window to allow
the air of judgement to flow out.

The Heart of the Matter

Midnight telegram and photo from J.D.'s old man
White-haired floater writing verse
Card collector with shifting gaze
Good morning argument
Hand on pit viper's shoulder
Skip and Joe with 63 feet of good time
Wrangle / dangle
U.A. female king fisher (37 lb.)
Waltz with Gravel's handshake
Soft-landing light lunches for Bia's
Vaudeville act: "strangulation demonstration"
Babe in arms, heart in throat
"May I help you?"
Time measured in feet
Feed me, I'm yours

Brenda Jean Hefty

The Liquid Body...

Needs to find its own level -
advice won't alter that
Feels its power, challenges the dams
Can change form, but always accepts itself
Knows it flows when well integrated)
(Knows it flows when well integrated)
Allows the bubbles of the past to surface
Hasn't a thought about vulnerability, just is
Glistens, especially in the dark
Distills its art

Its essential element is the ability to express love
Light is its mate and rainbows are their children

The Message

You called today.
It was difficult
to make a connection.
You were coming from a remote place,
a land of festering day dreams.

I was difficult to reach.
Out went my helping hand
and my desire to show you the way.
But the way I felt was - SEXY
at having an unexpected midday rendezvous
via the telephone.

Perhaps if you had said,
"Several hours south of Tokyo
there is a coastal hotel falling into disrepair.
At twilight an old man attends the rooms,
placing a kimono at the foot of each bed.
His passage through the corridor of
private bathing rooms is uneventful now.
He vacations in the past."

When you call again in such a mood,
ask for Aurora.
She comes from my inner fire.
She can read your mind and warm your heart.
She possesses the key to excitement,
and is more than fond of day dreams.

Brenda Jean Hefty

The Momento

Ending on a high note,
like flying from a trapeze,
takes faith in letting go,
and a love of the temporary.

A singer will tell you
smiling while singing opens the throat
and allows the highest notes
to escape with grace.

You and I chose to let go
at a high pitch, smiling and graceful,
with no communal "om" grounding us,
and no surrender to the mundane.

If flying, singing and loving
have a common thread,
it must be made of gold,
having been used by ancient seamstresses
to embroider the clothes of emperors.

Our needles are redefining its use.
We are constructing a garment
that will connect us at the heart like Siamese Twins;
designed to release our voices like uncorked champagne
and give us room to grow wings of desire.

Then, upon the night we are not together,
we will wear the garment in our dreams,
and with our hands on the trapeze,
we will leap into the air
and feel the high note forming.

The Panama Hat

Did you choose your own crown
or did it choose you?
Was it that southern sun streaming
through hanging moss on a century-old afternoon
which made the straw shade necessary,
or were you trading your life sign, the sun,
for the affections of one who thrives on
turning light into fire?

Not to be without one in the future,
you bought a duplicate, wrapped it in tissue
and placed it in the upper right hand corner
of your bedroom closet.
Does this insure the claim you have made on
the man you most want to be?

The tailor shares your dream of a white suit
to complete the picture you will include in
your portfolio. For you are an actor instructing
your avid pupils in the art of human behavior,
leading them further into chosen emotion.

Do you know you may be preparing the way that leads
to your own disorder as the applause crescendos?
Will you continue to trust the connection between
thought and feeling that produces the vibration
reaching your ears only an inch below the brim
of your panama hat?

The Pliant Husband

You remind me of mountains
Your staying power, the way
You sleep so soundly, the
Breadth of your shoulders
Speak of a weathered existence.

I Picture you at an earlier
Time climbing the rock faces,
Your boots steadying you in
An upward effort to greet
The view from the top.

You may have given up climbing
But, the minerals in your cells, tiny time
Capsules of ancient vegetation pressed
By tons of ice, breath a, whisper of
A relentless yet, peaceful life existence.

The Rainy Season

Big Daddy, a softball and two men
running over the warm, red earth.
She was pitching for the first time in five years.
She was the pivot, the fulcrum.
Was it the man's shirt she wore that
exposed her breasts as she picked up grounders?
Two more men arrived and it might have gone on
all afternoon, but they were going to the coast,
(he, she and the child).

He said it often as they drove, "What a beautiful day."
It had been raining for weeks, months.
The houses felt like sponges.
The earth had slid away from her.
The most graceful life in sight had fallen.
Was her soul too much to pay for a haven?
She had accepted the Piscean flow that had ignored
the dams and pushed her closer to the sea.
But the vision of a floating raft aflame woke
her each day.

As he shaded his eyes to look at the fire in the sky,
He said indifferently, "The rainy season is over."
The river would fall now, the raft would be beached.
But she wondered if it was faith or fate.
Does one stay on an isolated beach believing the
tide coming in has reached its height?
Even Noah used a dove.

She had refueled her own flame to light her way
and now she was learning how to design the perfect lantern
to enable her to travel even in the rainy season.

The Shape of the Heart

Does it absorb light?
Did a real craftsman mold it?
Do sea shells resemble it?
Will birds flock to it for nourishment?
Can it beat out a message in code?
Is it reflective and without blemish?
Has it recovered from being a pin cushion?
Is it recognizable in all of its forms?

Questions multiply when considering
the condition of the center of one's being.
How marvelous that the mind remains
curious about and grateful for the
mysterious generator of its own life force.

The Thoughtful Man

The thoughtful man leads a thoughtful life.
Trying to stay at home with his wife.
Something is calling from unknown spaces.
Calling from cool but longing faces.

Mysterious doubts play handball doubles,
As he sinks lower into jacuzzi bubbles.
Is his life ending or just beginning?
The strange thought has nothing to do with winning.

In a corridor he can't back out of,
It's up to him to find out about love,
discomfort is pushing, curiosity is leading,
while he holds onto a heart that is bleeding.

After using logic for an entire season,
He's about to declare, "How totally unfair."
The answer can't be simple, says his reason.

Suddenly, floating on an inner air
comes loves' soft voice saying,
"I'm here inside you where I always will be.
Simply stop defending yourself and you will be me."

Brenda Jean Hefty

The Veteran Trees

Billions of cells casting
a shadow on my life - you
were imposing yourself on
the space I am learning to
Possess.

I'll miss watching the squirrels
play on your trunk, but then
that was all I could see from the
first floor window on your side
of the house.

For three and a half years I
watched a shoe box shaped piece
of dawn from my bed on the second
floor as I gradually awoke.

Now that you're gone (8:14 tonight
you surrendered to the pull of gravity)
I realize what a vice I had been
living in; with one side removed
the breath comes easier.

Relief is what I feel, but not
without sadness.
I hesitate to go down toward the
river and look back - you won't
be there swaying ever so gently
and grandly.

He called you a class A bitch
as his chain saw dulled from
bits of metal imbedded, as if by magic,
in your thickness.
And he watched with calm resolve
as you fell, for you had pushed
his hour of triumph into the
night of the second day when he
had anticipated no more
than eight hours of labor.

To My Traveling Companion

Travelers - that's you and me,
Wandering the world independently.
Then suddenly thrust together
Like a bow to a violin,
Making music we hadn't planned.

Can we ever understand the why
Of a destiny that started with a lie.
As puzzling as love proves to be,
We can count our blessings and be thankful.
Joining our paths has created the best journey!

Travel Down -

Enter a wave
that is a world
of motion and power,
enough to take your
life if you resist.

Hanging in the balance
is your form of attachment.
<u>Trust it.</u>
It will sustain you.
And you will rise
to the surface.

As artist,
you see the multitude of choices.
As being,
there is only one,
And you have no choice
but to thrill to such freedom.

There Will Come a Time...

When I no longer twirl in my yard
with arms outstretched,
trees, branches and leaves
spinning in circles over my head.

A time when I no longer
make love in the afternoon
while listening to Spanish guitars
and violins, as bumble bees
flee their nest in the nearby woods.

It will be a time when
strange faces pass me in
the hall whispering hello
and goodbye at the same time.

When food is put before me
that I have little use or desire for,
and my bones feel like
they are sinking into my feet.

At that time my soul will
rise with such impatient
excitement because it
recognizes a path that leads
home.

Brenda Jean Hefty

VEDA REMEMBERED

There was something in the way
you held your pain that no one
gave you credit for.

I imagine you drank, but can't remember
if anyone in the family ever mentioned it.
Your smoking was obvious
and dreadful they said.

When you set fire to yourself
cousins talked about what
a terrible accident it was,
and blamed your physical handicap.

Yet you must have suffered little
compared to the years
of burning when you longed for
someone to touch, kiss and return
the look of love.

I always felt afraid of you
when we visited eyes that
had the power to make us
captives.

Reluctant and impatient,
I couldn't see the flame you
fanned in me, or know
I could live with such intensity.

I'll always remember you, Veda.
You burn with me.

Visitation By Invitation

Three men came to me today.
They were to be my judges.

Two had narrow eyes and olive skin.
The third was pale by comparison.

One spoke for the others.
He was the man of business,
experience and wisdom.
He was the oldest of the narrow eyes.

The younger one had answered
my invitation with compassion.
He was the man of softness,
knowledge and simplicity.

The pale man was there in body,
Like the third leg on a stool.
His mind was confused,
troubled and elsewhere.

They sat at my table.
They asked for my story.
They said they were sorry.

I told them as best I could
what had happened in our lives.
The way fate had embraced us,
gently removed our garments,
and placed us, on the doorstep
where sorrow is forever at home.

They said, "Show us where you stood
when the event took place,
and then we will leave you alone."

We walked single file
to the vine I had tended
while my daughter took flight
from my life.

What is Known by Heart:

A smile from across the room.
The air before a storm.
Childhood's simple melodies.
The taste of an apple.
A lover's touch.
The last breath of a pet.
The sound of a mate's footsteps.
All the smells life has to offer.

What is Your Zero?

Find that point, and you will begin a renewed life.
It is where everything begins.
It is the moment when you know you will not stop
Building the person you most want to be.

Without the zero,
There is no system of creation.
It is the means to an end.

Look to your dreams.
Search your inner space
When you are most quiet.
Your zero is waiting patiently.

YOU

You, the Collector.
Yes, you there in the book store
searching for images of subtle beauty,
always on the lookout for the unexplained.

You, the Dreamer,
who keeps externalizing the dream,
placing in neat stacks the invisible,
the true yearnings of our communal soul.

We trust you to be the magnet
for things scattered - moments of joy and pain
you then collage, coax and distil
into a fine essence we call your gift.

Having become the Giver,
you have created a habit you cannot give up -
incrementally poetisizing the world
with visions juxtaposed and offered
as the elixir to soften our hearts.

AFTERWARD

BY

Brenda Jean Hefty

We humans need the environment currently existing on the earth's surface. We refer to it, because observing and interacting with it reminds us that everything Is temporary, and constantly escaping our control.

Humanity has such a tendency to insist on its own permanence. We resist the idea that life goes on without us. Observing nature on a daily basis can be humbling and just what we need to keep things in perspective. If we let it, Nature and its constant evidence of death and renewal will tenderize us. When we pay attention to our natural environment we have the opportunity to truly appreciate the present moment.

Occasionally we see a creature crossing the street, landing in a tree or swimming across a pond that we have only previously read about or seen in photographs. It is such a thrilling moment. We feel awakened at that instant. Something that only existed in our heads becomes tangible. That moment tends to reduce our egotistical sense of superiority. The mystical reality of an armadillo crossing a agolf course fairway, or a great horned owl hooting for its mate, or a yellow rat snake making its way through the branches overhead causes us to catch our breath. This is their world too! We share a common habitat. We each pass this way briefly.

As we squash a spider who has found his way into the bathtub, we can't help but recognize the greater hand of fate that will eventually extinguish our own life. It is a telling event and uncomfortable as we realize how easily a life ends. No wonder so many of us become passi_vists, vegetarians, animal rights activists and keepers of the natural environment. It is painful to identify with callus destruction of any part of our ecosystem. Somehow we know our own demise is part of that loss. We are vulnerable. That vulnerability keeps us human and caring. Without it we might pave over most of our planet. (Aesthetics can be changed and rationalized.)

Protecting nature insures us of the continued stimulation and well-being of our vulnerability.

Knowing that life can be over in the blink of an eye not only causes us to be protective, but it also promotes creativity. When we are constantly aware that life is short and precious, we tend to motivate ourselves to do something, share something. We really don't like to be caught in a dull, unimaginative state. In fact, that is a state of mind that perhaps suspect, leads to suicide because a feeling of helplessness.

Another element of our need for and attraction to Nature and its unpredictable existence is that it is beyond our control. Whether we are vexed because we have a project that dement the reduction or removal of some natural elements, or we are trying desperately to preserve part of our natural surroundings, we have to admit we are not omnipotent when it comes to the well being of Nature. We often find that regardless of our efforts, Nature is an uncanny system. Take the peregrine falcon which most of us thought was doomed to extinction. Even with the reduction of harmful chemicals being used in agriculture, the fear was we were too late because the habitat was changing rapidly in a way that seemed detrimental to the falcon. However, much to our surprise, the peregrine flourished in areas of high-rise buildings because if found suitable nesting sites on the ledges of multi-story office buildings and condominiums. The bird didn't distinguish between cliffs and skyscrapers.

We may want to believe that we are the superior link, the thinker and leader of the natural world. However, if we are sensitive observers and honest with ourselves we will see that we are at the effect of the same elements as the rest of nature such as time, atmospheric change, instinct and fate. We are no more immune to the tenuousness of life than any other creature, plant or mineral. But we can enrich our lives by paying attention to the constant parade and performance of Nature. Our daily experience of Nature via our senses not only enhances our short existence, but also insures that we will contribute to the natural world in which we can thrive.

It would be enlightenting if we could review studies conducted on people who spend most of their waking hours out of doors versus people who are in rooms with few and small windows, artificial light and controlled heat and airconditioning. Would we see stronger immune systems in the former group? Would the latter group deal more with depression, anxiety and irritability? One telling piece of evidence is vacations people take. We tend to spend a greater amount of time out of doors when we vacation. The complexity of

Nature seems to be not only stimulating to our senses, but also soothing to our souls. It may be that vacations are not only necessary as respite from work and routine, but also as a revival of the suppressed psyche.

We still do not fully understand the effect sunshine has on the human body-like the energy transmitted to our skin when we sit in the sun, or learn the affect the natural world has on our well-being.

Perhaps the question is really "How could we live without Nature?" It would seem our own physical nature would have to change dramatically to do that. We are such an integral part of Nature- part of the food chain, even though we are mostly doing the eating, a keeper of the garden when we rise to the occasion. How many of us would choose to live indefinitely in a submarine or in an underground bomb shelter? Do we even have the capacity to do that?

I have found considering the question "Do we need Nature?" to be a wonderful opportunity to analyze the daily experience which I mostly take for granted and rarely question. Raising my consciousness in pursuit of the speculation has created feelings of wonder and gratitude for each precious and temporary moment that I experience my senses stimulated by the natural environment.

Everything is temporary and try as we might, we cannot gain full control of Nature. But our human nature can benefit daily from the interaction with and reverence for the uncanny, complex natural world we inhabit.

9 798822 943858